CATS SET IV

NORWEGIAN FOREST CATS

Nancy Furstinger
ABDO Publishing Company

visit us at
www.abdopub.com

Published by ABDO Publishing Company, 4940 Viking Drive, Edina, Minnesota 55435.
Copyright © 2006 by Abdo Consulting Group, Inc. International copyrights reserved in
all countries. No part of this book may be reproduced in any form without written
permission from the publisher. The Checkerboard Library™ is a trademark and logo of
ABDO Publishing Company.

Printed in the United States.

Cover Photo: Corbis
Interior Photos: Animals Animals pp. 9, 13, 15, 17, 19, 20, 21; Corbis pp. 5, 7, 11, 12;
    Ron Kimball p. 10

Series Coordinator: Megan Murphy
Editors: Stephanie Hedlund, Megan Murphy
Art Direction: Neil Klinepier

Library of Congress Cataloging-in-Publication Data

Furstinger, Nancy.
    Norwegian forest cats / Nancy Furstinger.
        p. cm. -- (Cats. Set IV)
    Includes bibliographical references and index.
    ISBN 1-59679-267-1
        1. Norwegian forest cat--Juvenile literature. I. Title.

SF449.N65F87 2005
636.8'3--dc22

                                                                2005040378

CONTENTS

LIONS, TIGERS, AND CATS

Today's **domestic** cats are relatives of the African wildcat. Ancient Egyptians tamed these wildcats about 3,500 years ago. They proved their value by keeping rats and mice out of the granaries where the harvests were stored.

Egyptians believed the cat was sacred. Anyone who killed this animal was punished by death. Sometimes, cats were buried in special tombs when they died.

Cats continued to be treasured throughout history. From Africa, people in Europe, Scandinavia, and North and South America began keeping cats as pets. Today, more than 40 different **breeds** of domestic cats exist worldwide.

Cats are clean animals. This mother lion licks her cub, much as a domestic mother cat would do.

Cats belong to the **Felidae** family. This family contains 38 species, including the lynx, the leopard, the tiger, and the puma. All cats stalk their prey. And, they all use their superior senses of sight, smell, and hearing for hunting.

Norwegian Forest Cats

Many people believe the ancestors of Norwegian forest cats served as mousers on Viking ships. For many centuries, these long-haired cats lived wild in Norway's forests. They later became prized for their hunting skills on Norwegian farms.

A Norwegian forest cat first appeared in a cat show in Norway in 1912. The first Norwegian forest cat club was formed in 1938. But, **World War II** interrupted the movement to preserve the **breed**.

These cats nearly became extinct due to crossbreeding. Fortunately, a Norwegian cat club helped this natural breed make a comeback. It did this by developing an official breeding program.

In 1979, the first **breeding** pair of Norwegian forest cats arrived in the United States. The **Cat Fanciers' Association** accepted Norwegian forest cats as a breed in 1987.

Skogkatt means "forest cat" in Norwegian. Norwegian forest cats inspired many Norse myths.

QUALITIES

The Norwegian forest cat is active and independent. These freedom-loving animals spent much of their history living in forests or on farms. So as a pet, they should not be confined completely indoors.

Norwegian forest cats are often reserved with strangers. But once they get used to a new person, they enjoy company. Sometimes, they select one special person to be their friend. They also enjoy being with other cats, dogs, and children.

The Norwegian forest cat's coat often makes it too warm. So during the summer, these lovable cats might not curl up in your lap. However, they demand chin scratches. And, they return the favor with affectionate head bumps!

Norwegian forest cats are skillful tree climbers. They also have been known to stalk fish in outdoor streams.

COAT AND COLOR

This forest cat has the full ruff, or fringe of hair around the neck, that is desirable in the breed.

Norwegian forest cats change coats with the seasons. In winter, a double coat keeps the cat warm and dry. The downy undercoat provides warmth. The long overcoat with its silky, flowing guard hairs protects against water.

In spring, Norwegian forest cats shed their winter undercoat. Their warm-weather coat is shorter and sleeker. Only their tail plume and toe and ear tufts remain all year.

Norwegian forest cats can come in every possible coat pattern or color combination. The most common are black-and-white or **tabby** patterned. Their emerald green or gold eyes sparkle like jewels.

The Norwegian forest cat's color will often affect
the thickness of its coat. Darker colors absorb more
of the sun's heat. So, dark cats have a thinner
overcoat with less undercoat. Sometimes, the coat
color will change with the seasons.

SIZE

The Norwegian forest cat is a large cat with a muscular body. Its hind legs are longer than its front legs. This raises the rump higher than the shoulders. Powerful legs and thick claws help these cats climb easily up and down trees.

Males weigh from 10 to 16 pounds (5 to 7 kg). Females are usually lighter, weighing 8 to 12 pounds (4 to 5 kg). Both sexes take about five years to fully mature.

The Norwegian forest cat's long tail is often the same length as its body!

These cats have triangle-shaped heads and straight noses. Their large ears are heavily tufted and set low on their head. Their large, expressive eyes are almond shaped and tilt up toward the base of the ear. They have long, bushy tails.

The tilted eyes of this Norwegian forest cat give it the impression of alertness.

CARE

Surprisingly, the silky coats of Norwegian forest cats do not tangle. So, they do not require a lot of grooming. This cat's winter coat sheds each spring, however. Grooming three to four times a week will prevent loose hair from tangling during this time.

Indoor activities will keep Norwegian forest cats busy. A scratching post lets them safely sharpen their claws. A climbing tree allows them to perch above the action. Toys, such as a ball or catnip mouse, bring out their playful nature.

Like all cats, Norwegian forest cats have a natural instinct to bury their waste. Your pet can be trained to use a **litter box**. Place the box away from your cat's feeding area, and clean it daily.

The Norwegian forest cat has a reputation for being healthy. Take your cat to a veterinarian for a yearly checkup and **vaccines**. The veterinarian can also **spay** or **neuter** your pet.

FEEDING

Make sure your Norwegian forest cat arrives in its new home with a bag of food. Feed it this familiar food. If you want to change brands, slowly mix in the new food to prevent your cat from getting an upset stomach.

Your cat needs a balanced diet. Commercial cat food that contains a good protein source, such as meat, poultry, or fish, should be on the menu. The label will advise you on how much to feed your cat based on its age, weight, and health.

Serve food and water in stainless steel, plastic, or ceramic bowls. Also, make sure your Norwegian forest cat has fresh, clean water. While many kittens crave milk, some adult cats are unable to digest it.

There are three kinds of commercial cat food. They are dry, semimoist, and canned. Kittens will need food that is specially designed for cats under one year old.

KITTENS

Norwegian forest cats are **pregnant** for about 63 to 65 days. A typical **litter** has about four kittens. When they are born, kittens are blind and deaf. They drink their mother's milk.

Kittens can eat solid food when they are three to five weeks old. At this age, they also begin to play. They can see and hear, and their teeth start to grow. By the time they are 12 weeks old, the kittens can join their new families.

Norwegian forest cats change before your eyes. Kittens boast long, woolly coats. But by three months, kittens appear short-haired. Only bushy tails hint at what's ahead. Sometimes, it takes two years for their coats to develop shaggy ruffs.

Like all kittens, Norwegian forest cats are playful, but they tire easily. It is important that they sleep a lot in their early months.

BUYING A KITTEN

Norwegian forest cats love toys. When adopting this breed, make sure you have plenty of things for it to play with!

Norwegian forest cats can live between 12 and 16 years. Once one of these cats chooses a human friend, it will bond with that person for life. It is almost as if the cat adopts the person rather than the other way around!

The Norwegian forest cat is a newly recognized **breed**. It is less common than other breeds, so it is harder to obtain. **Purebred** kittens can be purchased from breeders.

It is more difficult to find these cats through breed rescues or animal adoption agencies. This is because Norwegian forest cat breeders are often very particular. They prefer the cats be returned to them and not sent to an animal shelter.

Search for an active, alert kitten that glows with good health. The fur should be glossy, eyes bright, and ears and nose clean. If a curious, playful kitten prances over to play, it might be the one adopting you!

The Norwegian forest cat is often called a "wegie" for short.

GLOSSARY

breed - a group of animals sharing the same appearance and characteristics. A breeder is a person who raises animals. Raising animals is often called breeding them.

Cat Fanciers' Association (CFA) - a group that sets the standards for judging all breeds of cats.

domestic - animals that are tame.

Felidae - the scientific Latin name for the cat family.

litter - all of the kittens born at one time to a mother cat.

litter box - a box filled with cat litter, which is similar to sand. Cats use litter boxes to dispose of their waste.

neuter (NOO-tuhr) - to remove a male animal's reproductive organs.

pregnant - having one or more babies growing within the body.

purebred - an animal whose parents are both from the same breed.

spay - to remove a female animal's reproductive organs.

tabby - the striped or splotchy pattern of a cat's coat. A cat with this pattern is often called a tabby cat.

vaccine (vak-SEEN) - a shot given to animals or humans to prevent them from getting an illness or disease.

World War II - from 1939 to 1945, fought in Europe, Asia, and Africa. Great Britain, France, the United States, the Soviet Union, and their allies were on one side. Germany, Italy, Japan, and their allies were on the other side.

WEB SITES

To learn more about Norwegian forest cats, visit ABDO Publishing Company on the World Wide Web at **www.abdopub.com**. Web sites about these cats are featured on our Book Links page. These links are routinely monitored and updated to provide the most current information available.

INDEX